THE EXACT

TIMELESS AGES

KUMAR ABHISHEK

Contents

Contents

Contents

Preface

FOR ONCE AND ALL

The deep dark forest is never ending,

A long lasting river turns to the mountain,

To feel the snow and its aroma of freezing,

To let pass the forest in a darkest plain,

Now the river knows that the mountain will not let it pass,

But still the river try to rill its rock,

Trying times are hard but harder when gravity to encash,

It will twist the river in half and half make it crawl,

Yet the river find its way in eternity, however mountain stall,

The forest and mountains are not obstacle,

They are the face of the river to drill amd march towards destity to fall,

Upon the civilisation and vision of everlasting progress to the ocean for once and

all.

1. UMBRELLA OF SOIL

An ant bridge kindle behind umbrella of soil,
Visioned as kite of tree and mocking toil,
Having the breath of turmoil,
Passage of ant miracles, amplified and boil,
Serving ant analysed in tree rampage revenant,
Ant amorphous trilogy medieval may deterrent,
Painting the soil and devoid of stem,
A tree vista declare a war stern,
Visiting and map of swearing ants in the roots and leaves of tree to swim.

2. A HOUSEFLY STRIDE

A housefly stride to find dirt,
Ending up to find its eye with salt halt,
A mole often tries to impress listening my song,
Ending up to stunt like a stubborn bong,
A cockroach never try to fly,
Ending up to walk destiny on sly,
A dragonfly fly like a studd fly swiftly,
Ending up to make me laugh on it head like helmet nifty,
A lizard often try to teach me what should be,
Ending up to drag me to kitchen to make tea,
All trying to find ways of destiny,
Will find it or not is a question of treaty,
A bat swings in air to dent the dark,
Ending up to to spin around me while I walk,
A dirty dull grasshopper making decimal gaps,
Ending up to find life on digital shapes,
An orange cat come to me without permission,
Ending up to tell that he had tail without admission,
Mosquitoes don't come to bite me now,
Ending up to find some soul searching inside though,
An ant has finally got wings before dieing,
Ending up to find literacy in his state for reviving,
All anomalies are the distinct from each other,
Yet levying a common thing to find their Karma sooth and stir.

3. TURN AND TWIST

Democracy is what makes design
Of the people and trigger it to shine,
Like many elevation of different kind,
Democracy thrive to every circuit of mind,
Constitution is the holy book of it,
To constitute passages in every distinguished turn and twist.

4. BRIDGES

Have you seen the bridges,
It has a concrete floating in air,
Though the pillars freezes,
Every road sometimes float to dare,
In the suspension of University of ages,
Educating us to be dedicated and fair,
Life is full of bridges in stages,
To remind us to be learned and to share

5. DISTRACTED PATH

The crime against humanity is a distracted path,
Narges Mohammadi of Iran has no way faith,
Humanity needs to understand the way to renunciation is pernicious,
And full of trivial & testimonial times reckoning faith which is pious,
Let the hatred abolished & love become precious.

6. FORTUNE MAKER

Money could be a fortune maker,
But what takes it to be breaker,
Is important as it is feast to happiness,
That's why money tackles the steepness,
Of the life curves, which are diabolical,
Diabolical as it has uncertain goal,
Which makes it fragile, if you have money, have a ball

7. THE ARDENT FOCUS

The ardent focus on wild life is necessity,
Not only for the animals but the whole habitat like a treaty,
The basis dependence is not just life cycle but tended and trending dependence,
Such as animal and human both needs forests to exist and dominance.

8. REVENANT MOUNTAINS

Up and down revenant mountains,
Crabs in the hills track,
Books and hacks of meticulous,
Worthy heroics of fountains,
Permanent sky mat of night,
Checks the hatch kite,
Hidden maneuver of simple site,
Happen rampantly and historic height.

9. SYSTEM ANALOGY

Verse system analogy,
Chronicles of hampers hard,
Impact of satire vista,
Matter hard smarter ignites,
Yet are morphine of name and character,
Advocacy of shrine surrounding,
Meham victory of developed yearning,
Development of kindness in vivid character may mending.

10. SAVING DEMOCRACY FROM AUTHORITARIAN REGIME

Virtue sensitized the justice of narrow paths yellow fiction vehemently,
Non can violate gears of noting of heralded democratic pears of narrow white
pigeons.
Tether the sorrow and save democracy is the call vehemently made to justify the
near outcomes,
Nuclear design to save democracy nascent yet vandalising falsehood.

11. CLARITY OF FEAR

Gone are the days,
catching frogs in the pits of rain,
Gone are the days,
brunching fish with little bread grain,
Gone are the days
when rain soothes pain,
Now it captures the ongoing duty,
It rides the days to hinder daily life city,
Gone are the days,
When a little crab race in the basket makes us smile again again,
Now cars captures the imagination of people,
Bike rally in the traffic road in the rain become tool,
Gone are the days,
Amorphous ants walk makes us find us it's hoarded house frame,
Now everything looks familiar,
Nothing wonders us with sheer,
Now life is not an entropy adhere,
Gone are the days,
Now all around it is clearity of fear, it is clearity of fear.

12. MARIGOLD

The seasonal marigold are the color of eyes,
It brings the monotonous smell with swinging size,
The marigold often reminds me the besties of life like a prize,
Marigold of life, the life long friends, some soft some wise,
I find you Karti when life was in strife, now when it rise,
with you it never seizes, it goes on, it never cries,
You are the Marigold that defies all season with softness of zeal, always nice,
With you I found villages with going lows and highs,
Your marigold gesture defines your wordle puzzles like a morning fries,
Marigold thick softness absorbs all political socks, and drives,
You are one of the real shockers that absorbs all matters that politicise.

13. TRUTH: START AND CONCILIATION

Truth is the conciliation server,

It distil the dark, hate and traitor,

Truth is mystique and enigmatic,

Till it realises its circuit with dynamics,

It's dynamics are sobering ahead on path;

Path of light, resolve, concurrence with faith,

Truth is a big universal tree:a religion which starts self,

It can't be uprooted and planted cosmetically anywhere else, but or if,

Truth is triumph, it travels along with its infinite leaves and branches,

In evergreen environs or universal ocean of time and space avalanches,

Truth: start and conciliation, always find it's path in all circumstances,

It bridges the gap and advances, it bridges the gap and advances.

14. ALL THE BEST

Birds fly high in algorithm,
Our country is a wisdom,
Kite of tales have feathers of fusion,
India ever had a natural vision,
May the sky ever be higher in proud,
G 20 presidency makes us clear and loud,
The world is listening the song of new elevation,
Makes us vivid and firm in world wide devotion,
Technology and distinction is a new culture,
Testing the togetherness of our path and destiny,
One world, One Family, One future is the path ahead,
With the design of "Vasudhaiva Kutumbakam", well said,
Good Bye to all members of this journey who evaporate,
We will see you in Brazil in the next schedule that will inculcate,
The journey of earth must resonate every year and elevate,
The poet wishes you, " All The Best"!

15. FIGHT BACK

Every spectacle has a vision,
Every notion has a destination,
Manipur is burning alive,
May be its injury will recover and thrive,
But when humanity is at demolition&deprive,
Every contour&depression sought for change,
Change from helplessness, help from fringe,
Manipur is crying for alleviating its wound,
Which has deriving from the govt. own ground,
It is same as the frog and the Nightingale,
Where people are Nightingale,&frog is govt. with jingles,
The Nightingale is singing the song of mercy,
But failed&the voice cord distorted,
Distorted to cacophony of death, help and isolation,
Manipur is dieing out of compelling circumstances and inaction,
And the frog is teaching to sing better,
While Manipur is bleeding to caricature,
INDIA will fight for Manipur,
INDIA will retort to the cruel frog traitor.

16. OVAL WORLD

Oval world has oval transparancy,
The fiction is trident and the reality is fancy,
It revolve around money and trespass vacancy,
Oval world has everything but no innocency,
The politics of rigidness has covered decency,
The rich rejects the poor, are suffering in deficiency,
The hate mongers are in society doing cruelty everyday to see,
The more the oval world is spinning, the more it indulge in complex complacency.

17. KARMA OCEAN VIA ORNATE DEMOCRACY

Live Ornate of democracy are the bidding hour of weaving eclipse,
Middle of the hidden web of the huge shrine physical Universe,
Middle of the power of the power of man and physical vacuum,
Yatch of the world harmony and napping world of praise and symphoney,
Live ornate of democracy are the visible chemistry of the manhunt, shipyard of the
Karma ocean.

18. OBSERVATION DRAW THE CONGRUENCE OF MIND

Observation draw the congruence of Mind,
To the outer physical world of different kind,
I observe in a dream that ladders are the hanging boat,
In the space, there are many such ladders float,
Is it a approach or just a game of snake& ladder, fortune& fault?

19. LIFE IS ONE!

Life is one,
Make it fun,
Sadness undone,
Quality run,
Quantity in many ton,
Hurt non,
Loose gun,
Youth should learn,
Crime is to shun,
The earth spun,
Around the sun,
Time immemorial million,
Had won morn,.
Dews on flowers turn,
Sprinkled in crops of bun,
Who?I think the moon.

20. WHY STAR SHINES?

Why star shines?
Why are they called signs?
Why moon is yellow?
Why moon revolve & follow?
Star shines to showcase intensity;
There signs represent a bond to the earth or treaty,
Moon is yellow as earth's eternal fellow,
Moon follow as lonely, solo, so that earth can sought O.

21. GAME OF CROOKS

When it is game of Crooks,
It dealt with same type of books,
The tyrants bombs thrown by jumbos,
Make the hill in between crescendo,
The wars never look fair, Specially when it is from air,
From air everything looks easy, And volatile for target fizzy,
Our soldiers from land to land,
Are at real risk or are at real stand,
They not only bridge the gap of our total land,
But ensure and instill fear in their mind so that they not retort-rewind.

22. HIT WICKET!

A basketball player is drumming the ball,
He may not satisfied with his ability to throw and goal,
The net is too high to roll maybe frightened of height of pole,
He tried and tried again and shuffle but failed although he is tall.
A cricketer love to hit cover drive while he is drunk,
But he is short, not like basketball player who can dunk,
Once he missed to hit the cover drive and ball hit the stumps, he was duck,
He said empty promises are like curled hairs nothing, may be it is par score where
he stuck.
A footballar show red card for rough play,
Because his dribbling where too fast to resist the opposition's day,
Sometimes it is easy to score but not easy to resist the stay,
Sometimes it is easy to hit six in cricket, find hard to ground on the radicalised
clay,
Sometimes life goals remains like a basket, safe to shuffle then to goal in the tray!

23. WILDLIFE

Wildlife in India is in big distrust,
Their population is continuously decreasing without just,
Their life is important for the balance of ecosystem,
Animals often hunted for mere greed of skin, horns only to frame,
Could be stop just by spreading their inportance&kindness to them

24. RELIGIOUS DIFFERENCES

Religious differences are the setback for any country,
When religion become the tool of political weapon,
The most oppressed are common people &humanity,
Those involve in making differences often find fun,
And pity for that little religious excitement which is actually blind ego

25. CRIME

The country where crime become tool of oppression,
Land mafia, smuggler, property snatcher profession,
Are become the political hand of politicians of New India gimmick,
Has become new normal&later convert them as political pick,
In Opposition too, bahubali-you don't have to seek

26. POLITICS

Politics have become all about provocative speeches,
Political leader excite mass by reciting old&new tricks&ditches,
There are few leaders who speak truth to power,
There are more leaders who treat mass as lambs of rush hour,
The problem in Indian political system is its VIP culture,
Political leader think that they have possession on mass like vulture ,
Let us remind the govt. that that there welfare programs are like,
Sucking the blood of common man and supply when accident or need strike.

27. LANGUAGE

Language should not be the barrier,
Between human being as God has not send us with it to bear,
Like eyes, nose, mouth to see, breath & taste,
Language is artificial, that's why differ between state,
Be passionate for natural understanding,
Which makes one God's human being.

28. SUMMER

Summer season comes with the incessant heat,
This summer has raises the communal temperature hard to beat,
In these circumstances hand licking Desi food and village ponds to swim,
Are delight with fruits like mangoes, Kulfi and icecream.

29. INDIAN MEDIA AND HACKING OF MATTER

Role of media is to be a pipeline between budding information,
But in these time it has become the decision making station,
Media is even divided between party line,
It take a continuous stand for one political sign,
The height of hypocrisy is such that it elevates a non issue,
Like an Everest of information in favour of a perticular party view,
From regional to national to international affair,
DRIVEN BY MEDIA, IS UNETHICAL HACKING OF MATTER,
BUT STILL CALLED A RESOURCE FOR INDIA.

30. CREATE FOREST LIKE POETIC WIRE

Climate change is at alarming level,

Pollution is the cause & the main devil,

The root cause is not only govt's. failure but lack of individual responsibilty,

We are not aware of the root cause making excuse for weather insanity,

The need of the hour is individual practice by avoiding stubble burning to
checking vehicle pollution,

Govt need to regulate& control making stringent law to avoid industrial pollution
fusion,

Air, water& soil is changing into dumpyards,

If we don't stop today the day is not far when the earth will become only a
junkyard,

Small contribution could contribute a lot like growing trees also need govt effort to
replant after forest fire,

Forests are the lifeline,govt must also CREATE FORESTS LIKE POETIC WIRE.

31. RECIPE OF HUMOUR

Humour is an effective way for anything to let go...
It is the pearl which creates peace like a white flag,
Humour is a A.K.47 gun which targets ego...
And fire laughter in you in one round like blind shootout, zig-zag.

32. DEMOCRACY, THE TARGET OF SOME FANATIC GROUP

Democracy is the target of some fanatic group,
And retorting democracy, taking law&order in hand &are self proclaimed troop,
My defination of democracy is transfer of Power from people to their representative
constituting a system,
Where every state is abide by constituition,
federal structure&legislative wisdom,
And the national vision is of regulation and control over states in proportion,
Worthwhile alongwith the builder of national programme &international policy
vision,
I know everyone of you are aware of this&have the same defination,
But, time to reiterate it&remind the people representative of filthy aggression,
Time to let speculation&fear&draw attention towards FILTER OF
DEMOCRACY,
By the removal of fanaticism, creating vaccancy!

33. POLITICS OF OPTIMISM

Politics is a great amplifier of echoes,
Politics never ceases, actually it is about on &on like never ending prose,
Mahatma gandhi was doing politics of optimism,
Politics of optimism infers will to contain as well as release as a message,
That's why his message of wearing khadi, non-cooperation movement etc got popularity,
Like a morning light dissolves like stirring with a differentiated pigeon feather inside the earthen pot.

34. FASHION

Simplicity is the mark of distinct value,
It enhances impression as well as dense like tree, a airy venue,
That gives shade to pedestrians,
Our national machine should depend on simplicity to maintain & strain,
Growth must be inclusive w/expansion,
Like gas balloon flies in fasion.

35. STREAM OLD

Literacy in India is repetitive not idea based,
Swami Vivekanand had said that education must be idea based not
accumulatively trashed,
Otherwise librarians are the most intellectual in world,
An idea for it is differentiate education earlier & increase the particular stream
old.

36. TRANSMOGRIFIED

Mistakes are the transmogrified way of behavior,
Actually it is a sign indication nothingness of our inner sensor,
So never feel anything as it never happens and not truth,
Because Truth is the only bridge between God and human, too and forth.

37. THE DAHALIA OF OUR DAY

Songs are the delightful cup of coffee,
And ghazals are the romantic tea,
Folk music have a flavour of designated state,
Pop music are colourful sharbat,
These are the flowing wave around, daily,
Settle in our heart like jelly,
The nyctanthes of our night,
The dahalia of our day.

38. IF YOU WANT

Flowers are the divine&beautiful creation of God,
But thrones are too equally important to protect flower like a sword,
Thrones inspects each time someone come to plug flower,
These are the small natural power,
It is the tax to plug a flower from a plant,
If you want,if you want.

39. CRYPTIC AND EMBEDDED

In old days human being moved to states for trade,
Caused a lot of exploitation in the state where trade held,
British&European nations were disguised them to invade world,
Now the world has changed, Nation believe in eccentric trade,
Means countries are cryptic& embedded.

40. EXTREMISM, A PLATE WHERE ONLY BULLET IS SERVED

Extremism is a plate where only bullet is served,
Life there is like a falling meteor,
What we had seen in previous decade in Syria, Afghanistan, Namibia & many
more,
India is also not untouched by this inhuman activity,
Actually India is suffering this since independence,
Life has been continuously taken by terrorists in our J&K territory,
Either of the civilians or the armed forces,
Few Kashmiri youths are also misguided in trap of terror outfits,
They get trained and become ready to kill their own brothers&sisters,
This brain washing is ongoing,
Their are many resolution taken but the enemy breaks 'em all continuing its proxy
war,
The solution of Kashmir issue is in developing Kashmir&thus Kashmiryat...
Literacy should be the main channel not business&tourism,
Giving books to children w/o indulge 'em in selling kehva.

41. CLEANSING AGENT

Share market is the cleansing agent;
Cleans the waste either by elevation or descent,
In share market the data is collected, numbers are accounted,
Brokers get their brokerage through dealing in a manner, inherent,
People should invest here not to get money, but to money; invent.

42. TECHNOLOGY, BROADENING AND WIDENING

Technology is broadening& widening,
Money is also not without tossed& hardening,
Crypto currency is name given to this hot&attractive mercury,
These are the block chain based on instability of the market in hurry,
Cryptos should be future oriented like a growing peepul tree.

43. SAY NO TO INTOXICATION!

Youth of our country are misguided to take different kind of intoxication,
They drink liquor,smoke,chew tobacco, take drugs&chew different tobacco
production,
There is an urgent need to stop these production to scarce them as it is not good in
long run
As youth are indulging in these things in accelerating manner,this darken their
future and hence of our nation,
I know these are the things where the govt is getting the heavy revenue but at the
cost of our future recession,
And also loosing precious life of our citizen.

44. NIRVANA SHOULD

In summer season, the birds, stranded animals remain thirsty for a long time,
It is our duty that we should give them water & if possible some food,
As their adaptation is also developed w/ us & their life depend on us very prime,
My friends this is the path of Nirvana should

45. PETROL IS IN OUR MIND!

Obviously petrol is a liquified gold,

The raising price of it raising concern over future way of dealing with it,

It's scarcity is not actually real but disregarding and enrolled,

Because often we use petrol while wasting it without guilt,

The need of the hour is petrol&is saving it from further wastage through public awareness,

Surprise is we are caring about scarcity of water, is good but more scarce thing is petrol,

All the possible ways of reducing automobile pollution is symmetrical to save petrol i guess,

The thing is petrol is the the upper limit of automobile industry stall,

It is upon us to raise the limit to infinity and that is really possible through critically using it by just pursuing other method to release stress,

Petrol is in our mind we should propel without crawl.

46. FEAR NOT, I AM TRUE!

The earth moves around the sun it revolves,
It revolves,proves it's legacy to create views,
Sun is not greater than earth,it let not escape it from its crew,
Inside the freedom of humankind which let not removes,
Closing inner&out from its dream fuse, Fear not, I am true!

47. THE SKY TO THE OCEAN DOING HIGH FIVE

We human are agitated in the journey of life,
But look at the sky,
And the sollution that is aromatic, the ocean,
The sky to the ocean doing high five,
Look at the intense syrupy cloud,
Like a white spot of tea in the blue sky,
Look at the night stars,
Vigilant like a watchman,
Throwing a torch light to assure,
Everyone get a nap in its radar,
Look at the moon,
Ever changing shapes,
Sometimes full, sometimes like smiling lips, from the afar.

48. SELF DISCOVER NOT SELF RECTIFICANCE

Arrogance is a typical nature of human being,

Actually it come in one by the possession of something,

Something that has human value which create a feeling of superiority,

Or something which is rare induct arrogance sanctity,

One find it like a comparing tool of inner intactness,

Many find it to show it as a mark of success virtueness,

Arrogance is the killer of pride, which itself produce arrogance,

The thin line between self confidence/pride and arrogance is dangerous if not distance,

For the betterment replace arrogance with self discovery prior to become more humble lens,

As self discovery is the way to light and life while being humble would be self rectificance.

49. SMARTPHONE NEWS

This, the age of smartphones,
Creates a mode of clones,
Called social media bones,
A caricature made up of electronic zones,
Where one writes minds full grown's,
Engraved on the technical tones,
Today, smartphones are the memory ions,
That memorises life's all milestones.

50. MOON , BURNING BETWEEN THE LEAVES

Trees are given freedom,
Ballooning branches within confirms release,
Sky at the core so high with stardom,
Resonate the shine with fireflies;

The ballooning branches of the trees,
Illustrate the even silence of summer of a village,
The village called moon between the leaves,
Burning like flame of eternity before city, giving village privilege;

Pigeons humming sound like whistle,
Like chained in the gears of ears,
Startling sound create sizzle,
Like sky enlighten and thunders.

51. AI, THE FUTURE GUARANTEED

Artificial Intelligence is a precursor,

It consist of the brain teasers,

Puzzle are solved in the light of electronic tricks,

AI is the hidden boon to the world of geeks,

It is the innovation to innovate next generation,

It is the template of electronic world digging automation,

Its life depends on the AI environment platform philic,

AI can transform future into a advanced relic.

52. TO UNDERSTAND REALITY

Somehow I come to understand reality,
That PM Modi has a different royalty,
He always tends to sensationalize the matter,
He knows the nerves of people than anyone better,
He lightly targets the emotions which is the core of every relations,
Like the involved and evolved man suggested clouds can distract the radar of aviations,
Thus he targeted the emotions that Modiji is a all rounder supreme PM,
Who can even handle the tough and pressure better than anyone,
However frivolous the claim may be,
Modi ji among his follower remain and will be,
The psychology is very simple to digest,
That Modi is the result and portray of people's imagined leader who never exist,
Modi is the remainder of the India's growth story after 2014,
He got chance to be a people's leader but now the remainder has rotten,
Modi's popularity has come to a halt,
Modi, this time is unconfident and says everything with the pinch of salt,
Brand modi could not now capture the centre stage,
He has not now the hero of all hero image,
He has been decoded that he is only a one man & not a God,
He has been recorded that he is certainly the holder of failed record.

53. PLUS AND MINUS

A country can run only when,

Strong economy comprises and remain,

India is a subcontinent of uncertainty,

And economy not far to this conclusion and integrity,

India is the one big market of the world,

In almost all the economic activity of world our flag is unfurled,

With all the plus and minus that reflect our objective,

We are headed beyond critical point which makes it constructive,

In India any math that construct requirements of economy,

Is actually the plus which converge the life of scattered financial dummy,

In India, any math that construct deficit of the economy,

Is a dividing minus which causes fision during it's anatomy.

54. COLOR OF CASTE

Obstacles faced could be shorted out,
And colouring world could see the muted art,
God gifted life must be revolted while sorted caste,
And dissolve silently in this world of molten heart!

55. PAST IS A GOOD THING

Past is a good thing,

A nation is respected on account of its past,

A nation is credited on account of how it last,

Records are the channels where one can invent the future,

It is a like a tax applied to make future mature,

People say past is static,

But I believe it has momentum so dynamic,

Still I think past experience nurtures like pearl sac,

Remind me that the saline water needs tissue(sac) to become ornament of neck.

56. LIFE LIKE JUPITER'S RING, NO WING

Sometime we have to begin with nothing,
Or we have to search it before anything,
Like in Universe, not only the base or soil or something,
You need to find open space to stretch like earth's wing,
Only when one requirement is to be like having miniature of like Jupiter's ring.

57. INCOMPLETION

There is a story behind every soul,
This is called life in a role,
This life is tiny but whole,
Temporary in God's prison troll,
This life belongs to those who walks tall,
The wind of relief these days are install,
In the journey of templates, the temples are royal,
2020 a year of nature's disapprovals,
2020 a year marked very slow like crawl,
Now the elevation is like from forehead to top of the nosal,
Covid is showing its coloured enthrall,
A little negligence will hurt all,
The time for incompletion between pal,
Now the vision of incompleteness like coal,
Evolved in the pressure temperamental,
Everything has either two ends or circle,
One says start and end, other says the start and end at the same portal,
This is what Corona virus is if it has start then must have end-fall,
If circular then find the origin to be ended like wind-fall,
If it has life the end would be simple,
If it has strife the start is door free with handle,
Let's together and incompletion is the mantra to differ like coal-stall.

58. FACE OF BRAIN

Luck is a face of brain,
It has content to during strain,
Find the marks of past to invent future,
Assigned all work get lined to be pure,
Luck is not a unseen thing,
It is visible what lives bring,
Luck has wings,
Recognise it and get the feelings.

59. ADAPTATION REQUIRED

Indian economy is not remain the substantial one,

It has become a virtual pipeline world,

There is a elevation of data, extracting more data,

Data infers more data, and leads to data mining,

In this virtual data based economy, the pace need to be amplified,

Not only being with the speed it also need to be controlled or rectified,

But the original idea to make India a digital economic hub,

Is suppressed to feeling the forms to fileing IT, to banking system in public domain.

This half hearted approach is making India running slow,

We must involve our population as the bottom of economic activity in the pyramid,

Consumers are the faith of the economy,

China not only control it's consumers wish,

But also control consumers purchase power, liquidity, inflation, options and many such control,

Then China is able to say that they are a world leading economy,

Off course we are world power, we are the most patient(in general) country on earth,

I am also not saying we should control our consumers but involve them, make them aware of their rights,

Make them vigilant not like participation but patriotism,

And for this we have chosen the right path so far,

e-commerce is already have become a big event, we need to explore it more with open mind,

I mean to say don't control the consumer but the retailer, small businessman,

MSME's, cottage industries,
Not only for the nation's interest but also in the interest of MSME's
This provide immunity to buyers in a complete circle...
By providing MSME's a win win situation We could take care of our
people(consumer) of this beautiful country,
All I want to say is that we need to be more adapted to the digital era.

60. MISTER MIRACULOUS

Mr. Miraculous do things, after the miracle confirmed by the live watchers,

I don't understand this cheat(So Far),

They light on and up to do the black magic of lightening up,

It is not the time to error correction but if it exist I can smell the end of COVID,

To world,

Crunchy brain,

Twisted fan,

Life abandon,

From sanghai to London,

Torch views circular,

Everyday molecular,

Who knows mystery,

Behind chemistry

Lightening lust,

Frighteningly thirst,

Brighteningly worst,

Starting from crust,

Still a common man adjust,

with what hampering,

I am readily a personality of social distancing,

Thus I am not the common man,

And everyone fighting in the rain,

Is a fighter on its own,

I acknowledge akhbar distributed,

Bythose distributers these days stacked,

I am a published poet,

And my mumma-daddy says I am a hero.

Embracing Your Life

A Workbook for Modern Life

Rashmi Dixit

About the Author

Rashmi Dixit is an ICF-certified coach, leadership consultant, and facilitator with over two decades of experience empowering individuals to embrace their journeys with clarity, purpose, and intention. As the founder of *The Hive Consultants*, Rashmi brings a unique blend of deep empathy, cultural awareness, and psychological safety to her coaching and development work. Her expertise spans across leadership development, diversity and inclusion, emotional intelligence, and creating spaces where people can discover their authentic selves.

Inspired by her own personal growth and the rich tapestry of stories and connections she has gathered over the years, Rashmi's work reflects her deep belief in the power of vulnerability, mindfulness, and interconnectedness. Through *Embracing Your Life*, she shares insights, reflections, and practical tools to help readers navigate life's challenges and find meaning in every step of their journey.

Rashmi lives in Portland, Oregon, where she continues to create ripples of positive change through her coaching, facilitation, and community-building efforts.

Acknowledgements

Life has always felt like an invitation—a call to explore, to gather, and to dive deeply into the richness of existence. As someone who loves life, I have spent my years as a gatherer of people, stories, and experiences, some arriving through serendipity, others through careful design. Each encounter and experiment has been a lesson, a window into different ways of being, thinking, and feeling. This book is my humble attempt to share the insights, reflections, and lessons that have shaped me along the way.

This journey would not have been possible without the people who came before me and those who walk beside me. My mum, Smt. Usha Devi Pandey, my dad, Late Shri Ashutosh Narayan Pandey, my grand mum, Smt. Shivkali Dwivedi, and my grandad Rajaram Dwivedi are the roots of my existence, grounding me with their strength, resilience, and wisdom. They taught me to move through life with grace, courage, and an open heart. To my daughter, Aarna Dixit—your questions challenge me, inspire me, and constantly lead me deeper into my own journey. And to my son, Eashan Dixit—your innate compassion reminds me daily of the power of kindness and connection. You are my mirrors, my muses, and my greatest teachers. This book is also shaped by the love and companionship of my dearest friend and partner, Vivek Dixit. Your unwavering support and the quiet strength of your presence have been the steadfast witness to my journey, just as I have been to yours. You are the compass that guides me back to myself.

To my sisters—Shalaka, Jyotsna, Mansi, Sona, Heather, Kirsten and Bulbul—you have awakened my spirit and helped shape my philosophy. To my mentor, Sukhvinder Sircar, you have helped me learn the road to myself. Each of you, in your own way, has been a companion in my journey of thought and growth, sharing wisdom, insights, and laughter. Our bond transcends blood; it is woven from the threads of shared values and the joy of exploring life together. To my sisters bound by blood, Jyoti and Manjul, thank you for your enduring presence and connection. You are my family in the deepest, most cherished sense, grounding me in love and belonging.

To all those who have walked with me on this path, this book is for you. May it capture the spirit of the journey—the beauty in life's experiments, the wisdom in its challenges, and the joy in each unexpected turn.

How to Use This Workbook

This book is designed to engage your creative senses and it is more than just a workbook; it is a tool for self-discovery and transformation. Use it as a journal, a sketchbook, or a space to color outside the lines—whatever feels right for you. Every page is an invitation to explore your thoughts, express your emotions, and create your unique path forward. Follow the prompts, let your imagination flow, or adapt the exercises to suit your needs. This is your book to self-coach, grow with, and to make entirely your own.

A Workbook for Modern Life

 ## Part 1: Navigating Inner Turmoil

Chapter 1: Embracing Imperfection
Stories of self-acceptance and resilience, reflecting on poems about embracing flaws and finding strength in vulnerability.

Chapter 2: The Power of Reflection
Insights on understanding emotions, with stories about facing internal conflicts and turning them into growth opportunities.

Chapter 3: Facing Fears
Narratives on overcoming fears, illustrated with personal anecdotes of resilience and discovery.

 ## Part 2: Cultivating Peaceful Connections

Chapter 4: Harmony in Relationships
Stories exploring relationships, conflicts with neighbors, and finding peace through compassion.

Chapter 5: Empathy and Compassion
Essays and reflections on deepening connections through empathy, inspired by poems that highlight the beauty of understanding others.

Suggestion: Lead the way! Navigate through the maze of inner turmoil.

Part 1

Navigating Inner Turmoil

Chapter 1
Embracing Imperfection

In a world that constantly pushes for perfection, I've come to realize that the most beautiful aspects of life often lie in its flaws. Over the years, I've discovered the strength that comes with self-acceptance, and I want to share how embracing imperfections has allowed me to breathe easier and live more authentically.

A Story of Acceptance

One evening, as the sun was setting, I found myself reflecting on the small imperfections that I typically brushed aside or, worse, berated myself for. These were things that I had once considered failures—choices I might have handled differently, paths I hadn't taken, or words I wished I could take back. But as I watched the sun dip behind the hills, casting its uneven light across the landscape, I saw something profound: the scene before me was breathtaking, precisely because it was imperfect.

Just like that landscape, my life is marked by moments of roughness and asymmetry. And yet, in that realization, I felt a weight lift off my shoulders. I could accept that it was okay to stray from the ideal, to allow myself to be human. I began to see that these so-called flaws were not shortcomings but essential parts of my journey.

Strength in Vulnerability

I used to think that showing vulnerability was not okay. But as I embraced
my imperfections, I realized that vulnerability was, in fact, a doorway
to authenticity. By allowing myself to be seen—cracks and all—I invited
others to see their own flaws not as blemishes but as badges of courage. I
try to capture this sentiment in this poem:

> *A crack in my armor, a flaw in my plan,*
> *These are the spaces where the light can span.*
> *In the open wound, where hurt resides,*
> *Lives the beauty of life that none can hide.*

These words are an expression of how our vulnerabilities allow light
to enter our lives, illuminating parts of ourselves we might otherwise
hide. Embracing all parts of myself has been a crucial step in my journey
towards self-acceptance. I am still discovering parts that I had exiled or
that remain hidden, every day.

A crack in my armor,
a flaw in my plan,

These are the spaces
where the light can span,

In the open wound,
where hurt resides,

Lives the beauty of life
that none can hide.

The Freedom of Self-Acceptance

Embracing the interconnectedness of all things brings a profound sense of freedom through self-acceptance. When I understand that I am in everyone and everyone is in me—*Aham Brahmasmi*—I see that we are all reflections of each other, bound by shared experiences, imperfections, and potential. This awareness lightens the burden of self-judgment. In seeing myself as a part of the vast, interconnected whole, I am reminded that I am not alone in my flaws or my struggles. I am simply part of the complex, beautiful dance of humanity.

This insight allows me to approach self-acceptance not as a final achievement but as a practice. Self-acceptance is something I return to again and again, much like brushing my teeth each morning. It's not about reaching a state of perfection but about embracing my imperfect, evolving self each day. There are moments when I catch myself striving for an unattainable ideal, moments when I'm tempted to hold myself to impossible standards. But in those moments, I remember the sunset's beauty—a beauty that would not exist without the interplay of light and shadow, color and imperfection. Like the sunset, I am most beautiful not in spite of my flaws but because of them.

With each step toward self-acceptance, I find a growing freedom to be myself, to let go of the heavy weight of constant self-improvement and simply exist as I am. This freedom extends outward, too. When I embrace my own humanity, I become more compassionate toward others, recognizing that they, too, are beautifully flawed beings doing their best. This compassion allows me to approach others with patience and understanding, acknowledging that we're all navigating life's challenges together.

In this acceptance lies the liberation of letting go—the freedom of knowing that perfection is neither possible nor necessary. I am free to live fully, embracing each moment as it is and each person as they are, including myself. The freedom of self-acceptance allows me to release expectations and judgments, to engage with life as an unfolding experience of growth and connection, knowing that every small action, every thought, and every step carries the potential to create ripples of kindness and understanding in the world.

Suggestion: A wall of positivity and life. Fill in as you please!

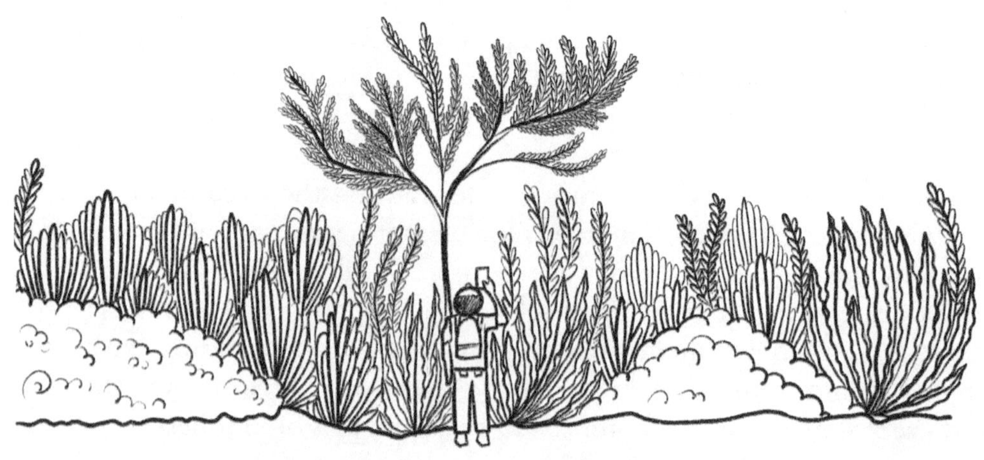

Self-Acceptance in Action

1. Letting Go of Perfection

Instead of striving for flawlessness in every task or interaction, there is a willingness to accept "good enough." For instance, you might complete a project with care and attention but resist the urge to overanalyze every detail. If a small mistake is made, instead of spiraling into self-criticism, you remind yourself that it's part of the learning process. This simple act of letting go allows you to move on with ease, focusing on what matters most.

2. Showing Up Authentically

In conversations and relationships, you no longer feel the need to put on a façade or pretend to have it all together. Instead, you allow yourself to be genuine, even if it means admitting uncertainty or vulnerability. You might say, *"I'm not sure about that,"* or *"I feel overwhelmed right now,"* without fearing judgment. This authenticity not only frees you but also deepens connections with others, inviting them to show up as they are.

3. Practicing Self-Compassion

When you experience setbacks or failures, you treat yourself with kindness rather than self-criticism. If you miss a deadline, fall short of a goal, or receive critical feedback, you pause to acknowledge your disappointment without letting it define your worth. You might remind yourself, *"This doesn't make me less capable; it's part of my growth."* With each act of self-compassion, you build resilience and inner peace.

4. Forgiving Others More Easily

With self-acceptance comes a natural compassion for others' imperfections. When someone makes a mistake or doesn't meet your expectations, instead of reacting with frustration, you approach the situation with understanding. You recognize that everyone is navigating their own challenges and extend grace rather than holding onto resentment. This creates more harmonious relationships and a lighter emotional burden for you.

5. Embracing Spontaneity

Accepting yourself as you are creates a sense of freedom to be more spontaneous and open to new experiences. You might try a new hobby, speak up in a meeting, or take a risk without worrying about the outcome. This openness allows you to experience life more fully and joyfully, unencumbered by fear of judgment or failure.

6. Seeing Mistakes as Opportunities

When challenges arise, instead of seeing them as setbacks, you view them as learning opportunities. For example, if a project doesn't go as planned, you reflect on what you can learn rather than dwelling on what went wrong. This shift allows you to approach each challenge with curiosity and growth, making setbacks less stressful and more enriching.

A mentor once said: Upset = Setup; any upset situation is an opportunity for learning and growth.

7. Releasing Control Over Outcomes

Self-acceptance brings a sense of ease in knowing you cannot control everything, and that's okay. For instance, if you're leading a project, instead of trying to control every detail and worrying about how others perceive it, you do your best and trust the process. This release of control brings a sense of peace and confidence in both your abilities and the journey itself.

8. Celebrating Small Wins

Rather than waiting for big achievements to feel validated, you begin to notice and celebrate small accomplishments along the way. Acknowledging these moments—whether it's a productive morning, a kind interaction, or learning something new—helps you appreciate the journey and reinforces your sense of worth.

9. Creating Space for Reflection

You take time to reflect on your experiences and how they've shaped you, honoring both your strengths and imperfections. You might set aside a few minutes each day to journal about something you learned or an aspect of yourself you're grateful for. This practice fosters a sense of self-acceptance and gratitude, grounding you in the present.

10. Building Resilient Relationships

When you accept yourself fully, you're able to form deeper, more resilient relationships with others. You don't rely on them for validation, nor do you expect them to be perfect. Instead, you approach relationships with mutual respect and support, creating a space where both you and others feel free to be authentic.

Self-Acceptance Within a Cultural and Collective Context

Self-acceptance within a cultural and collective context means embracing oneself as part of a larger tapestry, where individual identity is shaped by shared values, traditions, and ancestral wisdom. It involves recognizing that one's worth is intertwined with the collective's health and harmony, and self-acceptance becomes an act of honoring one's place within that collective. In many cultures, self-acceptance is not an isolated journey but a shared experience, reinforced by family, community rituals, and cultural practices that celebrate belonging and mutual respect. By embracing our unique qualities within the framework of collective identity, we deepen our sense of purpose, respect our cultural roots, and contribute to the overall well-being of our community. This interconnected understanding of self-acceptance fosters compassion and connection, creating a more harmonious and resilient society.

Reflection

Take a moment to sit in a quiet space and bring your attention inward.
Reflect on the following questions, either mentally
or by writing in a journal:

1. Awareness of Perfectionism

Are there areas in your life where you often find yourself striving for
perfection? How does this pursuit of perfection impact your sense of peace
and freedom? Reflect on what might happen if you allowed yourself to be
"good enough" in those areas.

2. Authenticity Check

In your relationships and interactions, do you feel safe to show up as your
true self? Are there any moments when you tend to put on a "mask" or
present an image? How might your relationships change if you allowed
yourself to be more vulnerable and authentic?

3. Practicing Self-Compassion

Think of a recent setback or mistake you made. How did you respond to
yourself in that moment? Consider how you might show yourself more
kindness next time, treating yourself as you would a close friend.

4. Connection with Others

Notice if there are people in your life with whom you tend to feel frustrated or impatient. Reflect on their challenges and imperfections. How might you approach them with more compassion, understanding, and patience?

5. Letting Go of Control

Are there situations in your life where you feel a strong need to control the outcome? Reflect on the possibility of releasing some of that control and trusting in the process. What feelings come up when you imagine letting go?

6. Celebrating Yourself

Think back on today or this past week and recall a small accomplishment or positive moment, no matter how small. How does it feel to acknowledge this win? Reflect on the impact of consistently celebrating yourself in small ways.

After you've reflected, take a moment to notice any insights or feelings that arose. Embrace these thoughts with openness, knowing that each reflection is a step toward greater self-acceptance.

Practice

To cultivate the freedom of self-acceptance in daily life,
try integrating these practices over the next week:

1. Daily Self-Compassion Ritual

At the end of each day, write down one small way you can show yourself
compassion for something that didn't go as planned. It could be as simple
as saying, *"It's okay, I did my best"* or *"I learned something today."* Notice how
this small ritual shifts your self-perception over time.

2. Authentic Communication Challenge

Choose one interaction each day during which you commit to showing up
authentically. It could be with a friend, colleague, or family member. Share
something honest about how you feel or think without filtering yourself.
Observe how this affects your connection with that person and your sense
of freedom.

3. Release Perfectionism Practice

Identify one task that tends to have you pushing for perfection. This week,
set a goal to complete it to a "satisfactory" level and then stop. Remind
yourself that it doesn't need to be perfect to be valuable. Allow yourself to
experience the freedom that comes with letting go.

4. Forgiveness and Compassion Exercise

Each time you feel frustrated with someone, pause and remind yourself
of your shared humanity. Take a deep breath, silently acknowledge their
imperfections, and then choose a compassionate response. See if this
practice helps ease tension and create more understanding.

5. Celebrate Small Wins

At the end of each day, write down one thing you're proud of, no matter how small. It could be as simple as getting through a challenging conversation, trying something new, or taking time to rest. Reflect on how acknowledging these moments builds a sense of self-worth and acceptance.

6. Letting-Go Visualization

When you feel the urge to control a situation or outcome, pause and close your eyes. Visualize yourself releasing control, allowing events to unfold as they will. Take a few deep breaths and say to yourself, *"I trust in the process, and I am free."* Notice how your body and mind feel after this practice.

7. Gratitude for Flaws

Each morning, list one thing about yourself that you often criticize and reframe it as a gift or learning opportunity. For example, *"My sensitivity allows me to empathize deeply with others."* Practice viewing your imperfections as integral to who you are.

By consistently practicing self-acceptance in these small ways, you'll begin to feel a greater sense of freedom and ease, not only within yourself but also in how you relate to others. Embrace the journey, knowing that each step toward self-acceptance creates ripples that touch every area of your life, leading you toward deeper compassion, connection, and authenticity.

Daily Invocations for Self-Acceptance

I am enough, just as I am, in this moment.
I accept my imperfections as part of my unique beauty.
I embrace my flaws with compassion and kindness.
I release the need to be perfect and honor my progress.
I am worthy of love and respect, exactly as I am.
I give myself permission to make mistakes and learn from them.
I am a work in progress, and I celebrate my growth each day.
I trust that I am on the right path, even when it doesn't feel perfect.
I release self-judgment and replace it with self-compassion.
I honor my journey and accept each step as necessary for my growth.
I am patient with myself and allow myself to grow at my own pace.
I am worthy of acceptance, both from myself and others.
I let go of comparison and celebrate my unique journey.
I am proud of who I am becoming, flaws and all.
I honor my feelings, knowing they are valid and a part of my experience.
I trust that my worth is not determined by my achievements or mistakes.
I am gentle with myself, even on challenging days.
I forgive myself for past mistakes and let go of regrets.
I am learning, evolving, and growing in beautiful ways.
I am grateful for the person I am today and the person I am becoming.

You don't have to be perfect to be whole. In embracing ourselves, we find growth, freedom, and peace. Life's most beautiful moments often emerge from our cracks, scars, and vulnerabilities—where true strength lives.

You may use **Harmony Deck Invocation cards** by Rashmi Dixit
and follow instructions on the card deck.

Suggestion: Take a minute.
What do you think you want to change in or around you?
What steps would you like to take to make that possible?

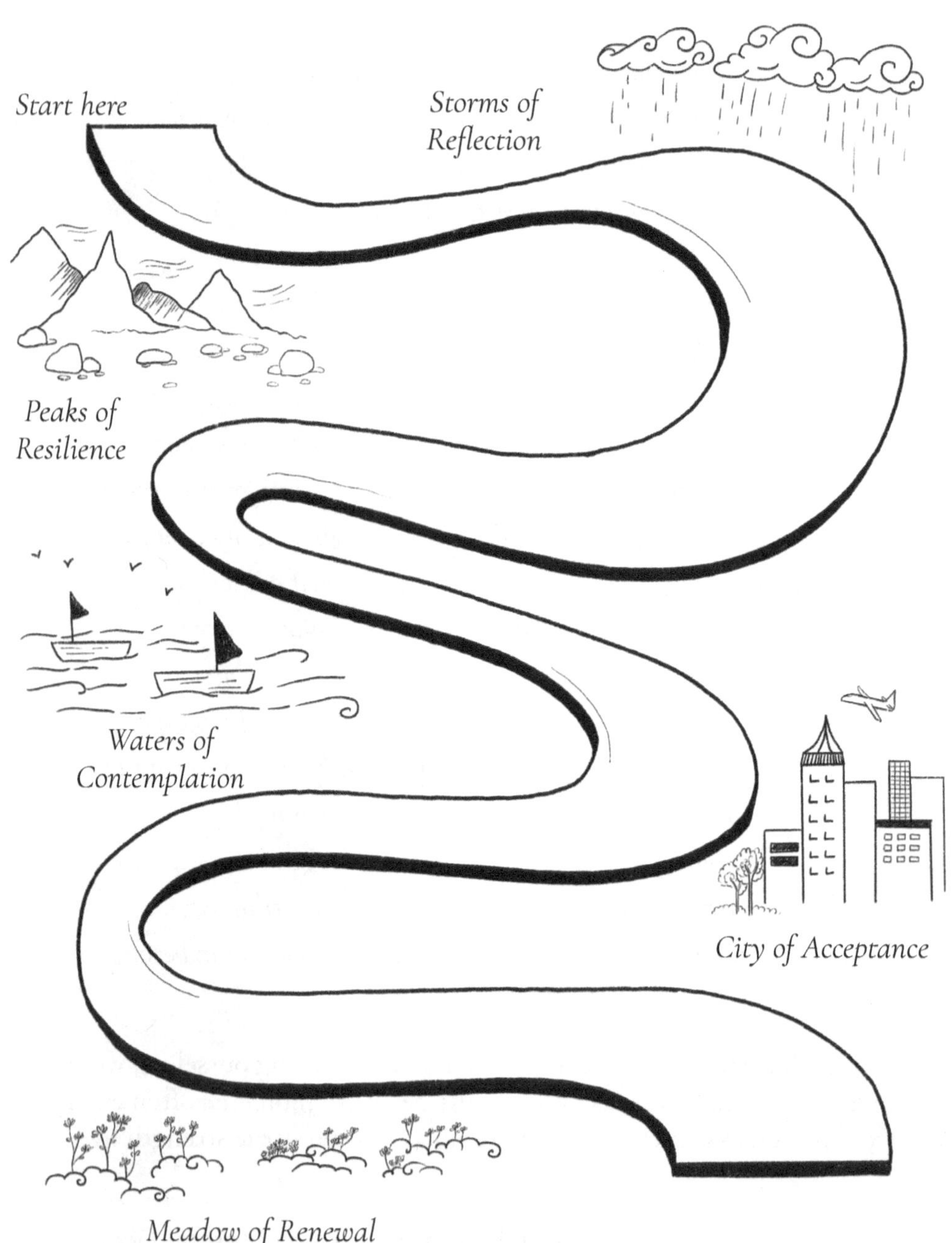

Start here
Storms of
Reflection
Peaks of
Resilience
Waters of
Contemplation
City of Acceptance
Meadow of Renewal

Chapter 2

The Freedom in the Pause – Embracing Self-Acceptance Through Reflection

Reflection has become my sanctuary, a place where I pause and find the freedom to choose my response. In the space of that pause, I am anchored in my values, able to navigate conflicting desires and emotions with clarity. By taking time to reflect, I've learned to embrace life's polarities—not as battles to win but as harmonies to balance. In this chapter, I'll share how the power of pausing and reflecting has helps me honor both sides of myself and find peace in the choices I make.

A Story of Living in Polarity

There was a time when I felt caught between two conflicting desires. One part of me craved the comfort and security of the familiar, while another part longed for adventure and new experiences. I felt torn, as though choosing one path would mean losing the other. Yet, when I paused and reflected, I realized that these desires were not enemies but complementary forces. Stability and change each held meaning and purpose for me; they were two aspects of a whole. As I leaned into the polarity, I saw that I could honor both values. By finding freedom in the pause, I gave myself permission to move forward with peace, no longer needing to reject one side of myself to embrace the other.

Understanding Emotions Through Reflection and Choice

Emotions are often our inner guideposts, directing us toward what we need to understand about ourselves. I used to rush past uncomfortable emotions, dismissing them as distractions. But by pausing to reflect, I began to see that even difficult emotions have wisdom to offer. For instance, when I felt resentment, I paused and asked myself what it was trying to tell me. I realized it stemmed from neglecting my own needs in favor of others'. This reflection helped me make the choice to set healthier boundaries. Each emotion I paused to acknowledge became an opportunity for growth and self-acceptance.

The Practice of Reflection and Pausing

Reflection, for me, is the practice of finding freedom in the pause. It's not a one-time act but an ongoing dialogue with myself. In moments of inner conflict, I pause, breathe, and ask myself simple yet powerful questions: *What am I feeling? What values are at play here? What would it look like to honor both sides?* This pause becomes a gateway, allowing me to choose a response that aligns with my deeper values.

Writing is one of my favorite tools for reflection. When I pour my thoughts onto paper, I gain perspective and clarity that often eludes me in the moment. Recently, I journaled about feeling insecure over a new project. As I wrote, I realized my insecurity was a natural reaction to stepping outside my comfort zone. By naming it, I was able to pause, acknowledge it, and move forward with confidence. In the act of reflection, I reclaim my power to choose and honor all parts of myself.

Take a minute. Pause. Breathe.

What is one thing that gives you comfort?
And one thing that excites or challenges you?

Reflect on how these elements coexist in your life.

Ask yourself:
How can I honor both?
What small step can I take to balance them today?

(You can use the space below to write.)

Turning Reflection into Freedom and Growth

In embracing the pause, I have discovered that true freedom lies not in eliminating inner conflicts but in choosing how to navigate them. Growth often exists on the other side of discomfort, and by sitting with my emotions, I find the strength to make choices that align with my highest self. Each time I pause, reflect, and make a conscious choice, I step closer to self-acceptance.

I invite you to take a moment to pause and reflect on your own experiences. What inner conflicts have you been avoiding? What values are calling for your attention? In the pause, you may find the freedom to choose a path that honors the complexity of who you are. Through reflection, we can transform life's polarities into opportunities for growth, learning, and self-acceptance.

Journaling Exercise: Navigating Inner Conflicts with Pause and Reflection

1. Identify a Current Inner Conflict

Begin by choosing a recent decision or struggle.
Briefly describe it in your journal.

2. Explore the Polarity

Divide the page in two. In one column, write down the values, emotions, or beliefs that support one side of the conflict. In the other, do the same for the opposing side.

3 Ask Reflective Questions:

What fears or desires are fueling each side?
How does each side serve or protect me?
How might embracing both sides help me grow?

4. Find a Path Forward

Reflect on how you might hold both sides.
What small steps or mindset shifts could help you navigate this polarity?

5. Set an Intention

Write an intention based on your insights.
For example, "*I pause to honor both my desire for stability and my longing for change, knowing I can choose a path that respects both.*"

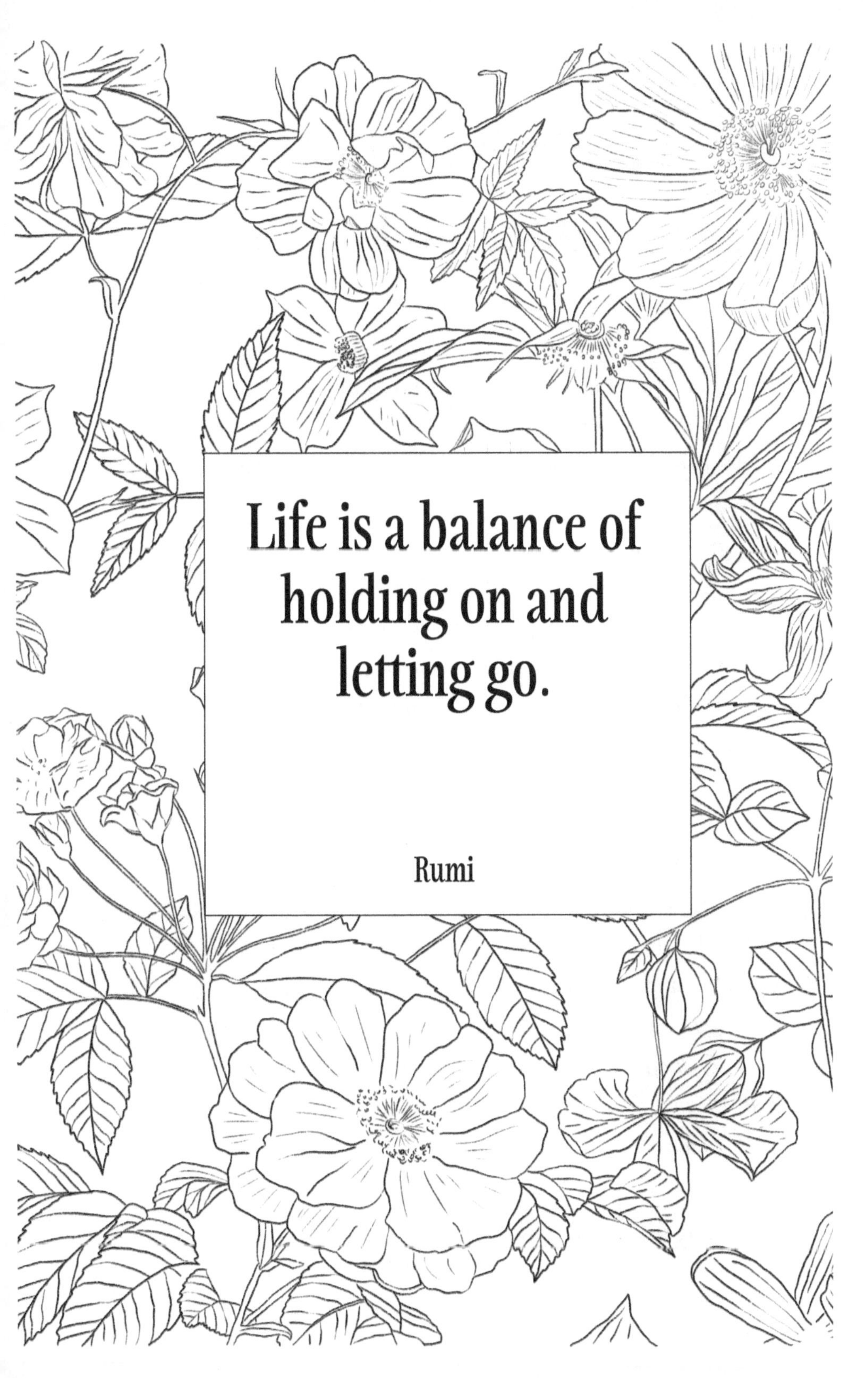

Life is a balance of holding on and letting go.
Rumi

Daily Invocations for Pause and Polarity

I find strength and clarity in the pause.

I honor both sides of myself, knowing each has wisdom to offer.

In the space of pause, I choose with intention and awareness.

I accept life's polarities and trust that I can hold both with grace.

I am anchored in my values, allowing me to navigate conflicting desires.

I give myself permission to pause and reflect before taking action.

I find freedom in the ability to hold multiple truths within me.

I trust that each pause brings me closer to my true path.

I embrace both my need for security and my desire for growth.

In the pause, I create space for compassion and understanding.

I release the need for a perfect answer and accept life's complexities.

I choose to see polarity as a source of balance and growth.

I honor my inner conflict as a path to deeper self-awareness.

In the midst of polarity, I trust my ability to find harmony.

I pause to connect with my inner wisdom and make choices from my core values.

I embrace the pause as a powerful tool for mindful living.

I am at peace with holding different perspectives within myself.

In each pause, I find the freedom to choose my next step.

I see conflicting desires as opportunities for growth and learning.

I trust the process, knowing that pause and polarity are part of my journey.

You may use **Harmony Deck Invocation cards** by Rashmi Dixit
and follow instructions on the card deck.

Chapter 3
Facing Fears

Fear is a constant companion, woven into the fabric of our lives. In today's hyperconnected and politically charged world, it functions as both a tool and a contagion—deeply personal yet collectively weaponized. It spreads rapidly, amplified by digital networks, media narratives, and social divides, seeping into our thoughts and shaping our decisions. For years, I let fear dictate my choices, mistaking its presence for control. But I've come to realize that overcoming fear isn't about erasing it—it's about learning to live with it, to move forward despite it. True courage isn't the absence of fear; it's taking that first uncertain step, heart pounding, unsure of the outcome, but stepping forward anyway. Through stories of resilience and personal growth, I hope to illustrate how I discovered my own courage by facing fear head-on.

The First Step Toward Fear

One of my most daunting fears was the fear of failure. I would replay possible scenarios in my head, imagining all the ways things could go wrong. There was a point when this fear stopped me from pursuing opportunities. I remember a particular moment when I had the chance to take on a challenging project. My initial instinct was to say no. The fear of not measuring up was overwhelming. But as I sat with that fear, I asked myself, *"What's the worst that could happen?"*

It was a simple question, but it shifted my perspective. I realized that even if I failed, I would learn something valuable. I decided to take the leap. As I worked on the project, I faced setbacks, but each time, I pushed through, finding resilience I didn't know I had. I took tiny steps toward movement. That experience taught me that the real victory was not in the outcome but in the act of facing the fear itself.

Finding Strength in Vulnerability

There's a unique strength that comes with acknowledging our fears rather than hiding them. I used to think that I had to appear strong at all times. But as I opened up to those around me about my struggles, I discovered a community of support. I remember a conversation with a close friend in which I admitted my fear of vulnerability. To my surprise, she shared similar fears. We laughed, we cried, and in that moment, I felt a sense of relief. By embracing my vulnerability, I connected on a deeper level with others, and I found that my fears were not as isolating as they once seemed.

In the face of fear, we often find,
Not a beast, but a mirror, kind.
Reflecting back what lies inside,
A place where courage and fear collide.

The Freedom of Embracing Fear

Accepting fear as part of life has given me a sense of freedom. I no longer see fear as something to avoid but as an indicator of growth. When I feel that familiar pang of anxiety, I remind myself that it's an invitation to expand beyond my comfort zone. By embracing fear, I've opened doors to experiences that I might have otherwise missed.

There's a certain magic in choosing to move forward despite fear. It's like stepping onto a bridge that you're not sure will hold yet trusting each step. Every time I face a fear, I gain more confidence in my ability to handle whatever comes my way. The act of facing fear has become a practice, one that has transformed my life in ways I never imagined.

Reflection and Practice

If you find yourself held back by fear, I encourage you to start small. Choose a fear that feels manageable and take one step toward it. Write about how it feels to face it, and remind yourself that every step forward is a victory. Over time, you'll find that the fears that once seemed insurmountable become pathways to resilience and discovery.

Facing fears is not about erasing them from our lives. It's about changing our relationship with them, allowing them to be present without letting them dictate our choices. By sharing my stories, I hope to inspire you to see fear as a friend that accompanies you on your journey, a friend that teaches you about your own strength and capacity for growth.

Part 2

Cultivating Peaceful Connections

Chapter 4
Harmony in Relationships

Relationships are essential to our growth, often mirroring parts of ourselves that call for deeper awareness. Over time, I've come to see that harmony in relationships requires a balance of compassion, healthy boundaries, and a profound understanding of peace. Peace does not mean mere compliance; it is the ability to create clear ground—a shared space where opposites can mediate, align, and navigate differences. Peace does not indicate weakness; it shows that I care. It is courage, resilience, and the power of pause. True peace resides in an interconnected space, flowing through moments and relationships in multiple directions, embracing complexity rather than a single path.

Creating Healthy Boundaries

Healthy boundaries are the foundation of peaceful relationships. They define the space between where I end and where others begin, honoring both my needs and theirs. Setting boundaries is not about keeping people out; it's about establishing a ground for mutual respect. I once found myself consistently drained by someone who expected my availability around the clock. To preserve my well-being, I needed to communicate my limits with both kindness and clarity, explaining that while I valued the relationship, I also needed time for myself.

Creating boundaries requires both assertiveness and gentleness. It involves respecting our own energy and choosing not to overextend ourselves. When I set boundaries, I can engage more fully, not because I am holding back, but because I am not depleted. In this way, boundaries become a form of peace—peace that honors both the self and the relationship, providing space to navigate differences with care and mutual respect.

The Role of Self-Compassion

To extend compassion to others, we must first cultivate compassion for ourselves. Self-compassion is a commitment to treating myself with the same kindness I would offer a dear friend. There have been moments when I was too hard on myself, particularly when a relationship did not unfold as I'd hoped. By practicing self-compassion, I learned to accept that I am doing my best, even when outcomes fall short of my expectations. This inner peace is not about perfection but about care—the courage to meet myself where I am.

Self-compassion strengthens my ability to set boundaries because it reinforces my sense of worth and the belief that I deserve balanced, fulfilling relationships. Through self-compassion, I recognize that peace also involves resilience, the courage to advocate for my needs, and the grace to accept imperfection. I am reminded that I am deserving of relationships built on respect and compassion, just as others are.

Finding Common Ground with Neighbors and People in Shared Spaces

Relationships with neighbors and others in shared spaces often bring unique challenges, but they also provide valuable opportunities to practice peace, boundaries, and compassion. I once experienced tension with a neighbor over a minor issue, yet the discomfort felt disproportionately intense. Reflecting on the situation, I realized that the conflict offered a chance to explore mutual respect and navigate the subtle power dynamics that can arise in shared spaces. Rather than trying to "win" or assert dominance, I saw the value in holding space for both boundaries and compassion. By approaching the issue with open communication and kindness, we were able to honor each other's needs, recognizing that neither perspective was inherently more valid than the other.

Navigating these dynamics requires an awareness of the give-and-take inherent in relationships and a commitment to equitable interaction. It means acknowledging when one person might feel marginalized or dismissed and taking steps to ensure that both voices are heard and respected. In doing so, we create a peaceful environment where differing needs and perspectives can coexist. The process taught me that mutual respect isn't about agreement; it's about understanding, accommodating, and fostering a sense of shared responsibility for the community space we inhabit. Through this experience, I found that peace, grounded in respect and compassion, can transform even small conflicts into opportunities for growth and deeper connection.

Guest and a Host

At the heart of relationships—whether with neighbors, friends, or strangers—lies the delicate art of being both a guest and a host. This interplay of roles calls for balance, respect, and an awareness of shared space. As a guest, it's essential to approach others' spaces and perspectives with humility and respect, honoring their boundaries and needs. Being a guest is about recognizing that we are temporarily part of someone else's world, and we must tread gently, listening more than asserting and being open to their customs and rhythms.

Conversely, as a host, we hold the responsibility of creating an environment of welcome and inclusivity, where others feel safe and respected. A good host does not impose expectations but instead fosters an atmosphere of openness and mutual respect. Hosting means setting boundaries that protect our own needs while allowing guests to feel valued and accepted. It's about navigating power dynamics thoughtfully, understanding when to lead and when to step back.

Mastering the art of being both guest and host in various spaces—whether physical, emotional, or relational—creates a foundation for meaningful connections. It's a reciprocal dance that demands attentiveness and grace, allowing both parties to feel seen, respected, and understood. In learning to be a gracious guest and a welcoming host, we cultivate environments where true peace and mutual respect can flourish, enriching every shared experience.

> *In every heart, a bridge awaits,*
> *A path that kindness cultivates.*
> *With gentle eyes and open mind,*
> *Compassion's peace is what we find.*

The Power of Compassion

Compassion is at the core of harmonious relationships. It is the bridge that allows us to connect with others without needing agreement or compliance. Compassion means stepping into another's shoes, seeing their perspective, and allowing peace to be a courageous act of understanding. This doesn't require that we surrender our own stance, but it does invite us to approach differences with empathy. This shift has transformed many conflicts in my life, turning them into opportunities for deeper connection and respect.

Reflection and Practice

If you find yourself struggling in a relationship, consider where peace, compassion, and boundaries might create harmony.

Ask yourself:
Am I honoring my own needs?
What boundaries would help me feel more balanced?
How can I practice self-compassion in this situation?

Peace is not simply the absence of conflict; it is a resilient space that allows differences to exist without discord, a ground for mediation, alignment, and mutual respect.

Through these experiences, I have learned that peaceful relationships require self-respect, clear boundaries, and a willingness to extend compassion both to ourselves and others. Peace is not weakness; it is the embodiment of care, courage, and the power of pause. This approach has brought me peace in my relationships and opened doors to deeper, more meaningful connections. True peace is multipolar, spiraling through different emotions and perspectives, honoring both the individual and the shared ground upon which relationships are built.

Chapter 5
Empathy and Compassion

Empathy and compassion are closely related, yet they can operate on different levels. While in chapter 4 I explored compassion as a response to immediate relationships, here I delve into a more conscious understanding of compassion that goes beyond individual interactions. This chapter reflects on cultivating a broader, more intentional compassion—one that embraces all of humanity and recognizes the interconnectedness of our experiences.

The Beauty of Understanding Others

Empathy opens the door to this elevated compassion by allowing us to deeply connect with others' feelings. When I truly see someone, I feel a sense of unity that transcends personal biases or judgments. It's about recognizing our shared human experience and allowing that understanding to guide our actions.

> *To stand in your shoes, to feel your pain,*
> *Brings warmth to life, like gentle rain.*
> *For when we see with eyes anew,*
> *We find that we're not so different, me and you.*

This poem is a reminder that empathy can lead us to a higher level of consciousness, where we see others as reflections of ourselves.

We find that we're
not so different,
me and you.

Empathy in Practice

I've come to view empathy not just as a feeling, but as a practice of opening my heart. It's a choice I make to be present with others, allowing their stories to touch me in a way that creates a ripple of understanding. This conscious practice elevates my connections, infusing them with a sense of shared humanity. When I listen without judgment, I feel the barriers between myself and others begin to fade.

Compassion as a Conscious Choice

This form of compassion is about more than just kindness—it's a commitment to recognize and honor our interconnectedness. I've experienced this deeper compassion through moments when I've set aside my own needs to genuinely support others. It's not about feeling pity or even sympathy; it's about recognizing myself in another's experience and choosing to respond with love.

> *In the quiet of a shared tear,*
> *We find that love is always near.*
> *No need for words, just a gentle touch,*
> *To show someone they're loved so much.*

At this higher level, compassion becomes a way of being. It's less about responding to each moment individually and more about cultivating a state of openness that we carry into all of our interactions.

Reflection and Practice

To engage with this deeper level of compassion, try seeing each person you encounter as a teacher. Reflect on what they may be revealing about your own capacity for love and understanding. Let this awareness guide your actions, allowing empathy and compassion to flow more freely into your relationships.

By cultivating this conscious compassion, we embrace our shared humanity, transforming our relationships and enriching our lives. It's a journey that leads not only to understanding others but also to a deeper connection with ourselves.

Chapter 6
The Role of Community

Creating a community goes beyond caste, creed, race, gender, sexual orientation etc. In *Hospicing Modernity*, Vanessa Machado de Oliveira critiques how modernity often reinforces individualism, leading to fractured communities. To build resilient, inclusive communities, we must look beyond these divisions and foster a sense of interconnectedness that values diversity.

Individualistic vs. Collectivist Societies

Individualistic societies emphasize personal achievement, which can sometimes lead to isolation and a lack of collective support. In contrast, collectivist societies prioritize interdependence, where individuals see themselves as integral parts of a larger whole. Reflecting on both, I believe that future communities can benefit from balancing these perspectives— embracing personal uniqueness while fostering a shared responsibility. This blend creates a communal fabric that supports both personal growth and collective well-being.

In individualistic societies, personal success often comes at the expense of communal bonds. People are encouraged to "do it alone," which can foster isolation and competition. In contrast, collectivist societies place value on community cohesion, interdependence, and shared resources. They emphasize that an individual's well-being is deeply tied to the well-being of the community. In considering these two models, I see an opportunity for future communities to draw on the strengths of both.

By celebrating individual contributions within a framework of collective responsibility, we create communities that are resilient and deeply interconnected. This balance fosters trust and mutual respect, allowing space for individual growth while grounding us in a sense of communal purpose.

In the arms of community, we grow,
Across divides, our purpose shows.
Together we build, together we thrive,
In shared humanity, we feel alive.

Learning for Future Communities

Future communities must consciously embrace interconnectedness. They should draw inspiration from Indigenous and collectivist societies, for whom sharing resources and responsibilities is a cornerstone of communal life. These cultures teach us that diversity strengthens the collective, enriching it with various perspectives and skills. Through this lens, we can cultivate communities that not only accept but also celebrate differences, making room for all voices to contribute.

To build a strong community, we must address biases head-on. This means recognizing the ways traditional structures may perpetuate exclusion and actively working to dismantle them. When we go beyond divisive constructs and seek to understand each other as human beings, we lay the foundation for communities that are united by trust and genuine connection.

Finding Belonging Beyond Biases

I've experienced the power of community that transcends these artificial boundaries. In one diverse group I joined, we found belonging through our shared humanity rather than our differences. When biases were set aside, we created a space where everyone could show up as their true selves. By focusing on what connects us, and appreciating and acknowledging our differences, we cultivated a sense of belonging that was rich, inclusive, and lasting.

A conscious community acknowledges that our differences—whether they pertain to race, gender, or any other marker—are not obstacles to be overcome but gifts that deepen our collective experience. True belonging arises when we feel seen and valued for our unique contributions and we see the same value in others.

Purpose Through Connection

Purpose in a community is amplified when it is inclusive and rooted in mutual respect. When I participate in communities that value diversity, I find that my connection deepens. Each person's perspective enriches the collective purpose, allowing us to achieve more together than we could individually. Letting go of biases opens us to a broader understanding of purpose, one that sees the community as a living, evolving entity.

Reflecting on my own journey, I see that community isn't just a place to belong; it's also a place to give. When I contribute to my community, I feel a sense of fulfillment that is rooted in our shared goals. By engaging in communities that embrace diversity, I've found purpose in knowing that I am part of something greater than myself—a collective effort to create a more compassionate world.

Suggestion: What have been some of your contributions to community?
How do they have a rippling effect?

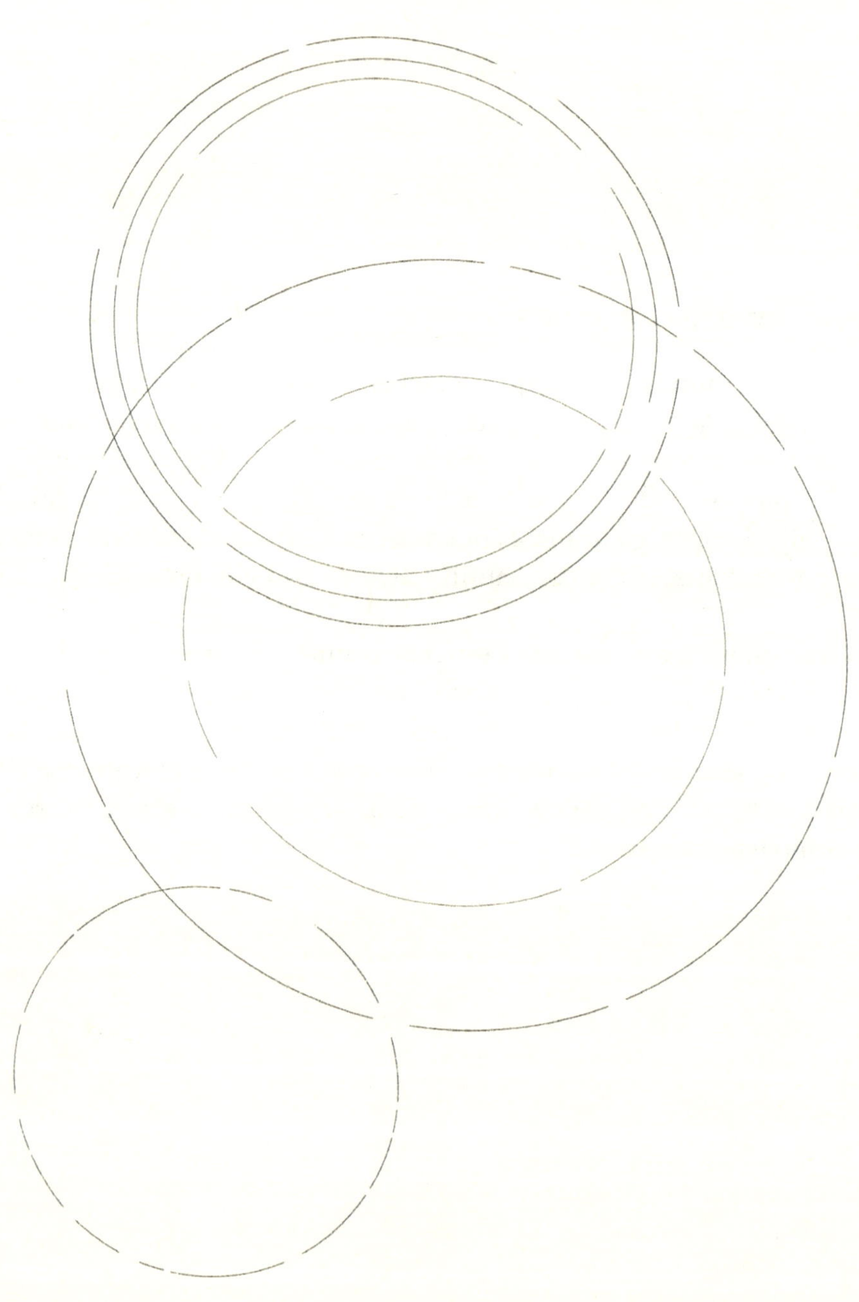

Reflection and Practice

To foster a conscious community, reflect on how your own communities might be limited by biases. Consider ways to engage with others that transcend traditional boundaries. How can you contribute to a more inclusive environment? By consciously embracing inclusivity and interdependence, we create spaces where everyone can thrive, laying the groundwork for future communities that are both resilient and deeply connected.

In such communities, we find strength in diversity, belonging in connection, and purpose in our shared humanity. By drawing on the wisdom of both individualistic and collectivist traditions, we create a blueprint for future communities that honor every person and see beyond division to the unity that lies within us all. Together, we can build communities that truly reflect our collective potential.

Chapter 7

Embracing Collective Consciousness – Honoring Our Interconnectedness with Animal and Plant Kingdoms

In the journey toward true collective consciousness, we are called to recognize that this planet is not ours alone. The animals and plants we share it with are not resources or scenery; they are our ancestors, our siblings, and integral members of the earth community. They were here long before us, teaching, sustaining, and embodying the wisdom of living in harmony with nature. Embracing this interconnectedness is about more than respect—it's about equity, humility, and a deep understanding that we are one small part of a vast and intricate web of life.

Learning from the Wisdom of Nature

Nature has always been a teacher to me—one that does not demand, yet offers infinite lessons when I listen deeply. From the resilience of a tree that bends in the storm to the quiet patience of a river carving through stone, the natural world holds the wisdom we often overlook in our hurried lives.

As Lao Tzu observed, *"Nature does not hurry, yet everything is accomplished."* This reminds us to embrace the flow of life rather than force outcomes. In our personal and professional lives, this could mean trusting the process of growth rather than constantly seeking immediate results. Just as a seed takes time to sprout, our dreams, relationships, and transformations require patience and nurturing.

Similarly, Indigenous wisdom emphasizes harmony with nature as a guide to sustainable living. The Lakota phrase *"Mitákuye Oyás'iŋ"*—*"All My Relations"*—reflects the idea that we are interconnected with all beings, not separate from the web of life. Similarly in Hinduism, *Vasudhaiva Kutumbakam* is a philosophy that suggests that all living beings on Earth are connected and share a future. It encourages people to consider the entire universe as a family, and to be responsible for each other and the planet, When we understand this, we begin to see nature not as a resource to be exploited but as a living entity that offers profound insights on balance, reciprocity, and renewal.

The Humbling Power of Interconnectedness

The deeper we explore nature's wisdom, the clearer it becomes that nothing exists in isolation. A single drop of rain nourishes the soil, which feeds the plants, which sustain the creatures of the earth. In the same way, our lives are intertwined with one another, forming an invisible yet undeniable network of relationships.

As Thich Nhat Hanh wrote, *"We are here to awaken from the illusion of our separateness."* In the modern world, where individualism often takes precedence, we can forget that our choices ripple out beyond ourselves. Whether in our workplaces, families, or communities, our actions shape the larger whole.

Consider a workplace where competition overshadows collaboration. When we adopt an interconnected mindset, we shift from "How can I get ahead?" to "How can we all rise together?" This shift fosters cultures of mutual support, trust, and shared success—much like the mycelial networks beneath forests that allow trees to communicate and sustain one another.

The humility that comes with recognizing our interdependence leads to greater compassion. When we understand that our joys, struggles, and destinies are linked, we naturally extend kindness—not only to others but also to ourselves. We learn to live in grace.

Reflecting on Our Impact

With the awareness of interconnectedness comes responsibility. If our every action affects the whole, we must ask: Are we contributing to harmony or discord?

Viktor Frankl, in Man's Search for Meaning, wrote, "When we are no longer able to change a situation, we are challenged to change ourselves." This speaks directly to the role we play in shaping the world around us.

If we pollute the environment, exploit others for personal gain, or act out of greed, we are disrupting the delicate balance that sustains life. Conversely, when we make conscious choices—whether by practicing gratitude, treating colleagues with fairness, or leading with integrity—we create a ripple of positive change.

Personal reflection is crucial here. Taking time to assess our habits, our ways of thinking, and our engagement with the world helps us shift from unconscious participation to intentional contribution. Journaling, mindfulness practices, or simply taking a walk in nature can reconnect us to this awareness.

Imagining a World of Shared Kinship

After learning from nature, embracing interconnectedness, and reflecting on our impact, we arrive at a powerful question: What kind of world do we want to create?

Martin Luther King Jr. spoke of "the beloved community"—a vision of society built on justice, equity, and love. Similarly, Buddhist teachings encourage the cultivation of metta (loving-kindness) as a force for healing and transformation.

A world of shared kinship is one where we see each other not as strangers but as family. It is a world where leadership prioritizes collective well-being, where organizations foster purpose alongside profit, and where communities nurture inclusion rather than division.

We each have a role in making this vision a reality. It begins with small yet profound acts—mentoring a young professional, standing up for fairness, making ethical choices in business, or simply being present for a neighbour in need. The possibilities are endless, but they all start with a shift in perspective: from separateness to unity, from scarcity to abundance, from fear to love.

As Rainer Maria Rilke reminds us, "The only journey is the one within." If we embark on this journey with awareness, humility, and courage, we become architects of a more compassionate, interconnected world.

And just like nature, there is no need to rush. We simply need to begin. Some say *What can I do alone?* It helps to remember that just as a single drop creates ripples across a vast ocean, one person's actions, no matter how small, can spark waves of change in this interconnected world.

We are here to awaken from the illusion of our separateness

Thich Nhat Hanh

Reflection and Practice

To cultivate a consciousness that honors our interconnectedness with
the animal and plant kingdoms, start by reflecting on your daily actions.
Consider how your choices affect the nonhuman lives around you. How
can you show respect for these beings as kin rather than resources? What
steps can you take to nurture these relationships and protect the habitats
they call home?

In this practice of mindful connection, find small ways to contribute to
the well-being of our shared world. Whether it's through reducing waste,
supporting conservation efforts, or simply taking time to observe and
appreciate the natural world around you, each act reinforces our kinship
with the earth. By approaching the world as a community of life rather
than a hierarchy, we build a foundation of equity, respect, and shared
purpose.

Through these reflections and actions, we honor our place within the
circle of life. We build a community that embraces the wisdom of all
beings, strengthening our shared consciousness by acknowledging our
responsibility and privilege to care for each other. Together, we walk
towards a future that respects every living thing as a relative, bound by
compassion, equity, and the timeless web of connection.

Suggestion: How have you been contributing to nature?

Part 3

Embodying Purpose and Presence

Chapter 8
Living Mindfully

Mindfulness has shown me how to embrace each moment with intention, purpose, and a profound awareness of the ever-present cycle of change. Central to this practice is understanding impermanence and letting go—a concept often intertwined with the idea of death. Death, in this context, is not only the end of life but also the end of moments, thoughts, and attachments. Accepting this has taught me to release with grace, allowing life to unfold in its natural ebb and flow, while appreciating time as it passes.

The Rhythm of Time and Letting Go

Mindfulness invites us to confront the impermanence of all things, including time itself. Just as each moment fades into the next, so too must we release what has passed to make room for what lies ahead. Through mindfulness, I've learned to see endings not as losses, but as essential parts of the natural flow of time. This perspective extends the concept of death beyond the physical, encompassing the transience of experiences and emotions.

> *Time drifts away like sand in the breeze,*
> *Moments we hold, then release with ease.*
> *For in letting go, we find our grace,*
> *Embracing each breath, each time, each space.*

In honoring time's transient nature, I've found grace in letting go. This process has brought a renewed appreciation for each moment, reminding me to live fully in the present rather than clinging to the past or fearing the future.

Time as a Guide for Purpose and Direction

Mindfulness also serves as a compass, helping me align my actions with a deeper sense of direction and purpose. When I'm fully present, I can clearly see where I'm headed and why. This is not about having all the answers but about setting intentions that resonate with my values. Living purposefully allows me to make conscious choices about how I spend my time, turning each moment into an opportunity to connect with my larger vision.

In my practice, I often reflect on how I'm using my time. I ask myself, *Am I spending my time on what truly matters?* This question serves as a guide, helping me prioritize and focus on what brings meaning and fulfillment to my life.

The Art of Presence and Intention

Mindfulness is intertwined with intentional living. By setting clear intentions, I choose how I want to engage with life rather than simply reacting to it. This intentionality brings focus and clarity, turning mindfulness into a deliberate art—an act of fully showing up, guided by purpose and vision.

Each day, I set a simple intention, whether it's to practice kindness, embrace patience, or pursue joy. These intentions help me stay grounded and ensure that my actions align with my true self. This deliberate approach to life transforms time from something to manage into something to experience, allowing me to cherish each moment as a unique opportunity for growth.

> *With each breath, I ground my way,*
> *In present time, I choose to stay.*
> *Intentions set, my vision clear,*
> *Time becomes a path, sincere.*

This poem captures how intentional living shapes relationships with time. Rather than rushing, I embrace each moment as an invitation to create, connect, and reflect.

Reflection and Practice

To live mindfully with purpose and presence, consider how you're spending your time. Reflect on areas where you feel attached or fearful of change, and explore what letting go might look like. Set an intention for how you want to move forward, seeing each moment as an opportunity to align with your vision and purpose.

Through mindfulness, I've learned to see time as a companion, guiding me to live with intention, presence, and a gentle acceptance of life's inevitable cycles. This practice has given me a deep sense of peace, grounding me in the realization that every moment is an opportunity to shape a life of meaning.

Chapter 9

Purpose Beyond the Self

Our sense of purpose extends beyond personal goals; it often finds its richest meaning in relationships and in service to others. I've found that nurturing connections with people allows us to grow in ways we can't achieve alone. Relationships reveal aspects of ourselves that remain hidden in isolation, helping us understand that our purpose is intertwined with the well-being of others and our communities.

The Growth in Connection

Relationships are powerful mirrors. They challenge us, nurture us, and push us to expand our perspectives. In my own life, I've seen how the people I love have inspired me to be a better person. Whether it's through family, friendships, or even brief encounters, these connections ground me and remind me that my actions impact those around me. Living with purpose means considering how my choices influence others and striving to leave a positive mark.

Purpose as Healing

Psychiatrist and Holocaust survivor Viktor Frankl introduced *logotherapy*, a form of existential analysis that suggests we find meaning through purpose. According to Frankl, even in the face of suffering, having a sense of purpose can help us endure and transcend difficulties. This approach emphasizes that purpose isn't just an abstract ideal; it's a powerful force that shapes our mental and physical health, the quality of our relationships, and the resilience of our communities.

When we cultivate a purpose beyond ourselves, we not only boost our well-being but also contribute to the health of our relationships and the strength of the communities we create. Research has shown that purposeful living can reduce stress, improve mental health, and even lower the risk of physical illness. When we feel that our lives have meaning, we are more likely to connect with others in positive ways, creating a ripple effect that benefits everyone around us.

Purpose in Relationships and Communities

Living with purpose goes hand in hand with fostering healthy relationships and building strong communities. By committing to something greater than ourselves, we bring inspiration to those around us. This purpose-driven mindset encourages collaboration, empathy, and mutual support, which are the cornerstones of any thriving community. When we bring purpose into our relationships, we lift each other up, creating an environment where everyone can grow.

For example, I once joined a community project focused on environmental sustainability. By working alongside others who shared a common goal, I felt a deeper connection and a greater sense of fulfillment. Through this shared purpose, we inspired one another to continue making a difference, reinforcing the idea that purpose strengthens not only our lives but also our communities.

The Importance of Inspiration

Inspiration is a vital aspect of purposeful living. When we inspire others, we ignite a spark that can lead to positive change. This is true not only for those who we directly impact but also for those that go on to influence others. Inspiration is a cycle that sustains purpose, creating a continuous loop of growth and contribution.

> *A light in the dark, a hand to guide,*
> *In purpose shared, our spirits glide.*
> *For in inspiring, we find our way,*
> *Together brightening each new day.*

By living with intention, we become beacons for others, showing that purpose can be both personal and collective. When we choose to live purposefully, we inspire those around us to seek their own meaning, contributing to a world where inspiration flows freely.

Reflection and Practice

To cultivate purpose beyond the self, reflect on how your actions impact those around you. Consider your relationships and communities—where can you contribute more meaningfully? How can you inspire others through your own purpose-driven choices? By nurturing these connections, we not only find personal fulfillment but also create a legacy of purpose that reverberates through our relationships and communities.

Through living purposefully, we discover a greater sense of self and strengthen the bonds that connect us all. In this interconnected web, we find that our purpose isn't just about us—it's about the collective journey we share. By embodying this truth, we contribute to a world that values purpose, inspiration, and meaningful relationships, enriching our lives and the lives of those around us.

Chapter 10
Continual Growth

Growth is a lifelong journey that requires openness to learning and a willingness to heal. Throughout my path of self-discovery, I've found that continual growth involves embracing change, seeking new knowledge, and allowing ourselves to transform. In this chapter, I share reflections and poems that celebrate the beauty of ongoing personal evolution and growth.

What does growth mean to you?

Use this space as your vision board for growth.

The Power of Lifelong Learning

To grow is to remain curious, to ask questions, and to explore new perspectives. Lifelong learning isn't just about acquiring new skills; it's about expanding our understanding of ourselves and the world. I've found that each experience, whether joyful or challenging, has something to teach. By embracing a learning mindset, we invite growth into every part of our lives.

> *With open heart and open mind,*
> *The world reveals what we may find.*
> *In each new lesson, truth is shown,*
> *Through every seed of growth, we're grown.*

This poem reflects how learning is interwoven with growth, reminding us that each step forward uncovers new layers of who we are.

Healing as Growth

Healing is an essential part of growth. It involves facing old wounds, forgiving ourselves and others, and finding peace in places where there once was pain. I've learned that healing is not a linear process; it requires patience and self-compassion. Each time I've allowed myself to heal, I've felt a sense of renewal that fuels my journey forward.

Through healing, we reclaim parts of ourselves that may have been hidden. We come to understand that our scars are not marks of weakness but symbols of resilience and strength.

The Journey of Self-Discovery

Self-discovery is an ever-evolving path, full of diverse landscapes and varied experiences. Sometimes, the journey is arduous, taking us along rocky roads where each step feels heavy. Other times, we find ourselves beside an ocean, watching the waves and feeling the vastness of our own potential. There are moments of breathtaking sunrise and moments when we feel worn and tired.

Through it all, this journey has taught me to appreciate my own unique path and to honor my pace. I've learned that I can pause, rest, breathe, and drink from springs of inspiration when they appear. I can choose to stay for a while, gathering strength, and move forward only when I am ready. In embracing this rhythm of rest and renewal, we allow ourselves to live more fully and authentically, honoring each phase of the journey as essential to discovering who we truly are.

The road unfolds, with steps unknown,
Through quiet fields and lands overgrown.
Some days we climb, with effort steep,
Some days we pause, in waters deep.
In rocky paths, or sunrise gold,
We journey on, both brave and bold.
To find ourselves, we take our time,
Rest when we need, and rise to climb.

This is a reflection on the wisdom of a journey that respects both movement and stillness, reminding us that self-discovery is not about rushing to a finish line but about honoring each step and pause along the way.

Reflection and Practice

To embrace continual growth, consider what areas of your life are calling
for learning or healing. Reflect on the lessons you've encountered recently
and how they've shaped you. By remaining open to growth, we allow
ourselves to evolve with each experience, building a life that reflects our
deepest values and aspirations.

In choosing the path of lifelong learning and healing, we embark on
a journey that is as rewarding as it is challenging. By honoring this
process, we uncover new aspects of ourselves and cultivate a life of depth,
resilience, and boundless potential.

Suggestion: Keep going and see what pattern emerges on the page!

What Next

Embracing Your Journey

As you turn the final pages of this book, think of your life as a journey—a garden you have tended with care. Each chapter represents a seed—some are seeds of self-acceptance, others of resilience, compassion, and purpose. Now, it's time to water those seeds, let them grow, and see what blooms.

Picture your path as a winding river, always flowing and changing course. You have navigated rapids of fear, drifted through calm waters of mindfulness, and connected with others along the shore. This river doesn't have an end; it invites you to explore new currents, discover hidden depths, and savor the beauty of each bend.

Your life is a canvas, and with each lesson learned, you add a new stroke of color. The masterpiece isn't finished, and it never will be. There will be moments of darkness and bursts of vibrant light. As you step forward, let your vision be the compass, guiding you through both the familiar and the unknown.

The journey of growth is endless, with each chapter building on the last. Whether you're cultivating deeper relationships, finding purpose in new ventures, or simply savoring the present, know that you have all the tools you need. Keep setting intentions like a captain steering through fog, trusting that the journey itself is the destination.

So, embrace the road ahead with courage and curiosity. You are the artist of your own life, the gardener who, with every step, creates a path that is uniquely yours. In this unfolding, you will find the wisdom, strength, and beauty of a life fully lived.

Sailing a Steady Course: Navigating a Life That Feels Like Home

Imagine your life as a sailboat, drifting on open water with the gentle guidance of the wind. Instead of racing to reach a distant shore or loading the boat with more than you need, you focus on creating a steady, balanced journey. Each choice you make is like adjusting the sails, catching just enough wind to move forward with purpose and ease. In a world that often pushes us to rush, accumulate, or seek constant new horizons, you learn to enjoy the quiet joy of simply sailing, anchored by the values that bring you peace and fulfillment.

Charting a Course That Feels Right

In a culture that encourages constant acceleration, it's a gentle act of courage to set your own course toward a life that feels "enough." Here's a calm and steady way to navigate, creating a journey that aligns with your values and brings you a sense of fulfillment:

1. Set Your Guiding Values as Your "Compass"

Think of your values as the compass that guides your journey. Choose three to five values—such as simplicity, connection, balance, or kindness—that help steer your course. These values keep you aligned, no matter where the winds may take you.

2. Choose Three "Destinations" Aligned with Your Goals

Define three main goals that resonate with your core values. Each goal is like a destination that brings meaning to your journey without rushing you. Choose goals that give your life purpose and direction, allowing you to enjoy each day on the way rather than constantly seeking more.

3. Map Small "Adjustments" to Keep Your Course

For each goal, identify gentle actions that act as small adjustments to your sails, keeping you aligned with your values without strain. Each action is a small but steady movement, helping you stay on course without needing to chase the wind.

4. Envision Your Ideal Journey, Not Just the Destination

Picture a journey where you feel calm, content, and at peace with the open water around you. Imagine what it feels like to sail through life with a sense of quiet purpose, allowing the journey to unfold naturally. This vision will remind you that fulfillment lies not in reaching a specific place but in navigating each day with care.

5. Pause for "Check-Ins" with the Horizon

Just as a sailor checks the compass and horizon, take time monthly or seasonally to reflect on your course. Are your goals and actions aligned with your values? Are you sailing in a way that feels balanced and true to yourself? These gentle check-ins help you navigate the journey with intention and ease.

By charting your course with care and moving steadily, you're creating a life that feels fulfilling and abundant, not because of how far you go, but because of the quality of each moment along the way. Instead of rushing toward an unknown shore, you're learning to enjoy the wind, the waves, and the rhythm of your own journey—a life that feels like home.